Mountain Redemption

Mountain Redemption

Nick McRae

BLACK LAWRENCE PRESS

Black Lawrence Press
www.blacklawrence.com

Executive Editor: Diane Goettel
Cover Design: Pam Golafshar
Book Design: Amy Freels

Black Lawrence Press
326 Bigham Street
Pittsburgh, PA 15211

Published 2013 by Black Lawrence Press, an imprint of Dzanc Books.
Printed in the United States

Contents

For Eric Smith

For there they that carried us away captive required of us a song; and they that wasted us required of us mirth, saying, Sing us one of the songs of Zion. How shall we sing the LORD's song in a strange land?
—Psalm 137:3–4

Drawl

I.

Sweet sorghum on a lover's tongue
Fresh briar marks on her thighs
Black beetles cased in cedar sap
          with new-hatched dragonflies

II.

A knife wound stanched with masking tape
A bin of cottonseed
One boy's fist on another's jaw
Bone shards in chicken feed

III.

What thoroughness   What cleanliness
An altar glazed with wax
Deer trails through the dark pine woods
Abandoned railroad tracks

IV.

On crumpled onionskin the words
          of Christ like sunburn scars
Liquor drawn from sweet corn mash
The black between the stars

I.

Thanatophobia on Shinbone Valley Road

Dearest fawn,
                half-crushed
on the pavement, forgive me.

Having found you already
dying, panting, feebly hoofing the asphalt,
unable to crawl away
from your back end—

limp, twisted, varnishing
itself in black-red,
hide gashed and mottled, light
fur thickly matted—

what my father once called *mercy*
I can't set my hand to,

can't raise the barrel,
send you leadenly into
the after, where nothing awaits us.

Life has been hard. It will yet be worse.
For this, I am sorry.

Yesterday, my father brought me
two halves of a rattlesnake—
one gripped by the rattler, the other
the head.
The pieces swayed in the wind.

This is what happens, he said,
and said nothing else.

This is what happens, fawn.
Nothing else.
I don't want to believe that.

The weather is nice today and it will be
a long time before I die.

Persimmon

As a boy, I built a trap for deer
from rusted tin and bailing twine
and rigged it up between the farm's
last two persimmon trees.
I'd seen the deer Dad strung up in the barn,
strips of hide and organs
strewn among the straw.
When morning came,
the shard of ruined tin hung lifeless
from its net of twine—
the trap untripped.
I laughed and breathed
and hacked the knotted cord
to pieces with my pocketknife,
then made a bed of leaves
and ate my fill of ripe persimmons.
Another day, my brother took his hatchet
to the two dark-wooded trees
and felled them both.
I watched as he dismembered them,
stripped the trunks and limbs of bark.
When Dad appeared,
my brother fled into the woods.
Dad swore. He stood silent
by the fallen trees, head down,
mouth moving as in prayer.
Side by side, we rolled the last persimmons
into piles then crouched beside them,
squeezed each tiny fruit—
some green and dry, some ripe,
some far too soft to save.

Mountain Redemption

When Ottis Wilkins lost his arm,
he burned his tiny sawmill down
then sold his long-dead in-laws' farm
and moved his family into town.
He opened up a barber shop
and hired his sons to sweep and mop
the place each day and brew coffee
for the men who came to see
the one-armed barber. Inch by inch,
the fresh-barbed rose up from the seat
like sinners from the mourners' bench.

Petunia Eckert's heart was broken
down and blown out like a tire.
The skinny girl she loved had taken
all Petunia's pluck and fire
and moved to Blue Ridge. Petie took
to church and, Sundays, wailed and shook
and made the preacher smile. That summer
Pete got work as a part-time plumber.
In basements she would flail her wrench
and watch rats, terror-maddened, clamber
like sinners to the mourners' bench.

Old Jackie Raburn didn't hold
with killing. Even the mice and snakes
that shimmied nightly over the cold
stones of Jackie's floors caught breaks

no other man would care to give them.
He had a shotgun, though, one trimmed
with etched brass plates. Some days he'd haul
the thing outside and discharge all
his shells at the ground and blast a trench
in it, then wait for silence to fall
like sinners to the mourners' bench.

Whenever Sherriff Biggers drank,
and that was often, he revved his Chevy's
engine up, sped past the bank
and dingy Main Street shops with a heavy
foot and siren wailing just
to see the townsfolk gawk as the rust-
and dirt-stained cruiser barreled by.
Once, he had to shoot a guy
to death. He watched the man's jaw clench,
his dead eyes lifted to the sky
like sinners' from the mourners' bench.

Preacher Greene, a handsome man,
a widower of just a year,
made all the married women fan
themselves and smile from ear to ear
when he preached of David's lustful pride
or the spear that pierced the Savior's side.
At home, the phone set off the hook,
he'd open to his favorite book—
Song of Songs—then feel the pinch
of chaste Paul's thorn as his fingers shook
like sinners on the mourners' bench.

And mountain people—hard as limestone,
rich as black silt, deep as clay—
dreamed each night of valley towns
where valley cornstalks stood up tall
like sinners from the mourners' bench.

For the Robinson Brothers of Chattooga County, Georgia, Now Deceased

Old women called the two's affliction *meanness*—
a word they usually saved for naughty children—
for these were Robinsons, not normal folk,
and couldn't help themselves.
                              In Center Post,
in Harrisburg, and far away as Gore
or Welcome Hill, god-fearing gossips clucked
and spun the brothers' mischief into tales:
one brother'd gone out whoring on a Sunday
while the other, drunk on cheap corn liquor,
fired his twelve-gauge at the Piggly Wiggly's
porcine marquee and, laughing, made the sheriff
chase him around the block until he spewed.

No one knew the brothers' Christian names
or which pine-dotted holler they called home.
Folks didn't know the older brother wept
when, on the radio, a preacher read
the Psalms, or that he played the fiddle deep
into the nights he once drank his way through—
and no one knew the younger brother'd lost
his wife to shine and almost ate his gun
a time or two.
                    But folks had seen their work,
the fly-swarmed carcasses of deer they'd poached—
the heads severed, meat unharvested,
hides marked with a shaky, knife-scrawled *R*.

Take, Eat

We skimmed the bottom of Duck Creek for crawdads,
sifted through the silt with our fingers,
felt the cool rush of fright as the tiny claws curled around us.

We held them up to the low light,
saw the glinting points of reflection,
shell the color of Georgia mud.

My brother grasped the heads between his fingers,
pinched them off with a wet pop, strung them as bait on his line.
We carried the bodies home with the few small fish we'd caught.

I had never eaten crawdad before.
Our neighbor fished them from a boiling pot with tongs,
husked them of their shells, soft as infant fingernails.

The tail meat floated in a pool of butter,
the white muscle curling in on itself.

I ran from the house into the pine thicket,
kicked pine needles into muddy heaps.

I leaned hard on a tree as thin as a cow tail,
stepped on the trunk, waited for the damp snap,
the acid gasp of its breaking.

Deacons Meeting

Five men smoke outside the convenience store
that doesn't exactly have a name. Over the door
hangs a sign: COLD BEER CHEAP GAS.
The men smell of hay and cow and hot skin.
Two perch on a tailgate, their boots
barely scraping the gravel.
One wears a damp red hat and he lifts it
to wipe sweat from his balding skull with a rag.
The one in the white t-shirt swears
and says, *hell hath no fury like a woman's scorn,*
that's what the Bible says, and the one
beside him disagrees, reckons it's not even in the Bible.
The hell it ain't, the other says, because he knows
it's a good one and all the good ones
come from the Bible. The sun pours out wet heat
like a steam engine and the ground
radiates and the hood of the truck shines dully,
reflecting in the eyes of a hound
whose tongue lolls and who hogs
the only bit of shadow cast by an old turnkey
Coke machine. The older one gets to explaining
how that ain't necessarily so when high above
in the hot sky a jet breaks the sound barrier
with a jarring crack and the five men and the dog
crane their necks upward to figure out
where exactly it's flying to. *I bet that sumbitch*
is headed to Warner Robbins, one of them says.
Naw that's north it's headed, says another,

I betcha it's headed to Chattanooga,
and the shirtless one with the stubbled jowl
who has until now been silent
figures it's about damn time they talked about
something else besides women.

Beheaded Carcass of a Deer

We cannot know its pilfered head
with velveteen antlers. And yet its hide
is still imbued with heat from inside
like a living thing, though now it's hours dead.

Otherwise the steam would not still rise
from the neck's stump; the blood pool wouldn't grow
in a widening ring like a red-black halo
on the leaves before my and my father's eyes.

Otherwise our nostrils wouldn't flare
with hate so fresh and mournful, as the deer's
must have flared when the poacher's shot rang out;

when the bullet split the morning air;
when from the woods the deer's death caught our ears.
We drag it homeward: silent, sick, devout.

II.

Pessimist's Guide to Miracles

A donkey in Siena brays the name
of Catherine, his saint, but no one hears—
no Balaam to be spared the angel's flame.

How many miracles pass by this same
irreverent way? We're sleeping off our beers
some Sunday while a donkey prays the name

of some Italian saint. We watch the game,
the infomercials' half-time racketeers,
flipping past the preachers' sulfur, wrath, and flame,

all while the donkey's keeper, in bed with shame—
with someone else's wife—gondoliers
his way to hell, moaning the vessel's name.

The donkey's voice is sweet as aspartame
and Catherine leans down to rub his ears.
We're blind to her, we Balaams, blind to flame,

but hey: we die. We all do. Life is lame.
Miracles can't save us from our fears—
a whirlwind singing its next victim's name,
a storm-split oak, a farmhouse wreathed in flame.

St. Nicholas of Lycia, Defender of Orthodoxy, Wonderworker

In Turkey they scarcely knew my name—
Father, they called me. *Bishop*. And every day
they came to me one by one and spilled
their sins in the dark, spat their own damnation
through the slot, my dim face on the other side.
The other priests were the worst.
Forgive me, Father, I dream of her on my mouth
like grapes, wake to the taste of wine.
They never asked me if I wanted their sins,
never asked my name, but I took them all
nonetheless, baked loaves for the poor
from the heat of them, scattered them
like rye seed over the rectory's sandy garden.
When the famine came, they slowly forsook me,
their stomachs too empty to sin. Only the butcher
still came to confess. Every day he entered my booth
to offload himself, the load a little bigger each time.
Forgive me, Father, I have doubted.
Forgive me, I have fornicated in my heart,
with my hands. Father, I am hungry.
When he told me of the three little boys,
how he split their flesh from bone with his cleaver,
laid them in salt to cure like swine, I knew
there could be no forgiveness for me, for him,
for any of us. I tore my vestment from my body,
ran bare-chested into the streets purpled by dusk.
Inside the butcher's shop I laid hands on the barrel

of boy meat and brine, plunged them into
its cooling depths, felt their names on my skin,
I swear I did. People like to say I prayed for the boys,
that I cinched my sainthood in a matter of seconds,
three miracles in one as the boys sprang from the barrel
clean and whole and blinking like new foals.

Isaiah

With blistered lips and tongue I prophesied
the coming fire, the blight, the trampled vineyard,
the kingdom overrun.
                              Looking inward,
I'd seen the nightmares of my heart collide—
seen famine, my people in captivity
while I, my condemnation wrought in verse,
was too unclean to speak. And even worse,
I'd seen my name fall to obscurity.

I placed the coal upon my lips—I'd say
an angel did—to cleanse me of the wrongs
for which my unwashed people burned.
                                          With songs
of grape and ash, I gathered scribes and preached—
through bandages—the price they'd have to pay.
They trembled. That's how deep in them I reached.

Of Solomon

Beloved:
>*Lover, dark as I may be*
>*from picking sun-sweet, nectar-heavy fruit*
>*in other vineyards, give yourself to me.*
>*My bed is fertile. Tend my withered root.*

Lover:
>*Mind your fruit, your drooping vines.*
>*I've seen whole packs of foxes stalking through*
>*your open gates. Catch them. Crush their spines.*
>*Forget them. Then I'll give myself to you.*

Beloved:
>*I was in the streets all night,*
>*helpless to my body's single need.*

Lover:
>*I was busy drinking starlight*
>*through my skin—the wheat fields thick with seed.*

Friends:
>*If love's a cellar, bolt the door.*
>*If love's an apple, bite it to the core.*

Nicolas of Antioch, the Proselyte

Acts 6–7

We were waiters, the seven of us,
anointed by Peter and the others

to feed the wives of martyred Greeks.
Stephen was our leader, and how beautiful

he was. His beard gleamed like smelted copper
in the heavy sun as we gathered wheat.

His shoulders moved like a weaver's
hands beneath his thin white robe.

I thought of the old stories, of Leda
taking the swan's warm, firm neck

in her hands and laying it across her lap.
I thought of feathers on damp skin,

the honk and flap of urgent love,
her tongue trailing the curve of his beak.

Mornings I watched as Stephen stirred
heaps of ash and coal to wake the fires

within the hearths we'd built together
from mud and clay and days of sweat.

When they killed him, I crouched among the stones
to hold him, kissed the place his face had been.

Genesis

It may have been a whim on which the world—
the universe—was spoken into matter.
Then we happened and made ourselves the master
of it all—the beautiful and gnarled
collection: root and flesh, baleen and feather.
And it may have been an accident that cast
us all from Paradise into the grassed
and dying fields to hunger, kill, and weather.

But separate as we were—the rise and fall
of towers and tribes, our languages confused,
the rocks we lay our heads on lashed to spears—
we found a covenant in the green sea's swell,
the cypress with its windy voice, a bruised
body entwined with ours, our numbered years.

Samson in Love

… out of the strong came forth sweetness.
—Judges 14:14

He always imagined grasping
his father's blade, running it hard

down his own scalp and jaw as his hair fell
about his feet in messy piles.

He thought of plunging his arms
elbow-deep in the wine jars,

rubbing the bitterness into his skin
until his hands were pruned with violet.

When he saw the Philistine girl,
he swore he knew how he would end,

swore there would be whole days
dozing naked in empty fields,

his head resting in the small of her back,
her shoulder blades looming in his eyes

like Zion and Arafat, and as he climbed them
with his fingertips he'd dream

of God transfigured and wake to it.

Nicholas Copernicus

I wanted to wrap myself in the crisp green
of the priesthood, feel the gentle bend of the host

before its breaking. I wanted to open myself
like a scroll and cant the ancient algorithms

of salt and oil, of vinegar and blood and forgiveness.
I wanted to fill gilded halls with homiletics

and whisper absolution in the dark.
But the tilt of the sky turning above me

seemed too imperfect, the slope of the stars
along the horizon bent too sharply toward the earth.

How my hands shook as I raised the astrolabe
and spun its dial—how damp with sweat

the parchment I scribbled equations onto.
Nights, in fields like open doors, I turned my ear upward

to hear the stars' confessions: *We are distant, we are vast.*
Forgive us, Father, though we burn already.

III.

Psalm 137

Where now are the old men of my childhood
        who laughed, swore, jawed plugs of tobacco
        and spat the red-brown swill into the dust
        while their wives lined pews and threw their bodies
        on the altar, wailing, *I will cling to the old rugged cross*
        and exchange it someday for a crown?
Where are the men who pressed through briars
        and barbed wire, scoured close-grown pine woods
        for winter calves, heaved the bleating beasts
        onto their shoulders and trudged through frost
        as hot piss trickled down their backs?
Where are the young men who, elbow deep in grease,
        leaned, blackened, into the shells of Internationals,
        knuckles bloodied, and tooled the cast-iron carcasses to life?
Where are the boys who strung up two-point bucks
        by kerosene light, sliced the creatures throat to groin,
        and flushed out the steaming viscera?
Where are the children who squatted by creeks
        in dark pine thickets, hovered over the waters,
        dragged their fingers through loose silt,
        feeling for the delicate forms of crawdads and tadpoles—
        who tore through briars with wild abandon
        and sprang forth bleeding, laughing, swatting mosquitoes
        from their necks and picking burrs from their hair—
        who, bodies light and scrubbed red, dozed through hymns
        and sermons on thick-aired church days and woke
        to the sobs of old women while the organ droned?

Where, O Lord, is the home I only almost had—
        mythic, bloody as a psalm in the mouths
        of old and dying men who will take it
        with them wholly when they go?

Joseph Van Gilreath (1924–1991)

> *Having a live coal in his hand, ... he laid it upon my mouth,*
> *and said, Lo, … thine iniquity is taken away.*
> —Isaiah 6:6–7

Back from the war, he married
a church girl. Together, they worked
his father's farm until the farm

wouldn't pay, then both took jobs
in the carpet mills that sprang up
like pokeweed across the Georgia foothills.

She called him a tall drink of water.
Long and lithe, he towered over everyone,
though all in those parts came

from the same Scotch-Irish stock—
all Gilreaths, Hoods, McRaes, Littlejohns—
all stooped and copper-haired.

Once he doused a cigarette
on his wife's tongue as, eyes closed,
she stuck it out at him. Weeks later,

the razor hook of his carpet knife slipped
from its work and sank into his eyeball.
He called it his just deserts.

For years, when he fell asleep in his chair,
his glass eye open and glistening as he snored,
he scared the life out of his grandkids.

Like Christ, he was always watching.
On a hot Tuesday, while his old International
idled beneath him, his heart seized.

They found him in the fresh-plowed dirt,
his good eye staring at the sun,
the glass one half-buried in the earth.

Killing a Rattler

At first, the double-barreled shotgun blast,
and then the dull, wet thump and metal clank
the snake made as he dropped it chunk by chunk
into a pail. With eyes clamped shut, I'd missed

the kill. I felt a rough hand clasp my wrist
as his tobacco wafted close: *Boy, think
before you walk out here alone.* The stink
of blood and gunshot ripened as he passed

the pail beneath my face. I'd heard of snakes
the size of a man's leg, been taught to steer
away from brush and dark thickets. I squealed

as Grandpa palmed my forearm like an axe.
He thrust my hand into the cooling mire
of meat and scales then held me as I bawled.

Cozy Manor Personal Care Home, LaFayette, Georgia

The room's too hot and reeks of piss and puke
and lemon bleach. Paw Paw's flannel robe's
stained gold with weak iced tea, his cuff's hem frayed,
picked ragged by his untrimmed fingernails.

The nurse tells Dad he wet the bed again,
says he shakes and hollers in the night
and half the time they have to strap him down.
She says he'll barely touch his collard greens,

his buttermilk and cornbread, honey-softened
saltine crackers—but that he's doing fine.
Every time we leave, Dad doesn't talk
for hours, just grips the steering wheel and stares,

and when he speaks he begs me for his life.
Don't do that to me, son. Don't never do it.

Gutting the Farmhouse Upon Grandfather's Death from Alzheimer's

My heart leapt when I thought
       of all I could destroy.

I tore the cherry banisters
       from the foyer's broad staircase

and piled the splintered dowels by the door.
       Dad ripped piping from beneath the sink.

The hollow copper rasped and clanged
       as he dropped each length of pipe at his feet.

He raised an axe, cleaved
       each cabinet door from its hinges,

and hurled the ruined wood through
       the window frame he'd emptied with a sledge.

I swung my old claw hammer
       and pierced the drywall.

Jaw clenched, I hammered
       until my arms were rubber,

then followed the floor's vibrations to the pantry
       to watch Dad hoist his sledge and laugh,

smashing the shelves to splinters,
       his eyes full of sweat and rapture.

Orpheus in Huntsville, Alabama

My mama, godly as she was,
never forgave my daddy for quitting
the church. For politics. She couldn't.
She'd always wanted to marry a preacher,
and married one, but then he ran
for mayor and won. The king of Huntsville.

Years later, when her mind was gone,
she told me how he'd lay her down,
his fingers circling her bellybutton,
breathe the scripture into her neck—
*Thy navel is like a round goblet
which wanteth not liquor*—and take her
with biblical authority.
She said that, once he'd shed the cloth,
his touch no longer felt the same.
How could it? He forsook the Spirit.

Now both of them are long buried.
But daddy taught me the fiddle, and mama
sang her hymns so sweet they shimmied
out her throat and into mine.

Apple

A man finds an apple in an empty field,
no tree for miles, only fescue, ankle-high,
yellowed with sun and drought. He holds
the green fruit to his face, smells its tart musk,
feels on his lips the skin's fine grit,
the heat of evenings trapped in its meat.
He thinks of the quince trees he dreamed
under as a boy, stacking the pale fruit,
bulbous, splotched, hard as river rock,
into fragrant pyramids he could topple
with a finger, how he spent whole summers
calculating their paths as they spilled
like seed across the patchy ryegrass.
He remembers the first tooth he lost to one,
a quince, when he first tried for a bite,
remembers the small tearing sound,
the acid taste of blood and fruit, the shock
and then the cool relief as his gasp drew
wind across the wound. But there are no
children in the field, and this sun is nothing
good to dream under, so the man decides
to go on his way. At first he places the apple
like an egg back on its bed of grass,
but then he sees the peel's faint freckles,
the stunning blackness of the shadow it casts
on the turf. He squats before the apple,
lays hands on its warm weight, head bowed,
imagines the bite he would take, feels it sour
in his cheeks. Handful after handful,

he tears the spiny grass from its roots,
parts the soil's black jaws. He rolls the fruit
into the wrist-deep maw, presses sod
down over it, lies upon it bodily, his ear
to the ground, strains to hear it growing,
to hear the deep shade that will bloom
any moment, any moment, surely it will.

Acknowledgments

Grateful acknowledgment is made to the editors of the publications in which many of these poems originally appeared (sometimes in slightly different form):

American Literary Review—"Apple"
Birmingham Poetry Review—"Genesis," "For the Robinson Brothers of Chattooga County, Georgia, Now Deceased," "Mountain Redemption," and "Joseph Van Gilreath (1924–1991)"
Copper Nickel—"St. Nicholas of Lycia, Defender of Orthodoxy, Wonderworker"
Country Dog Review—"Gutting the Farmhouse Upon Grandfather's Death from Alzheimer's"
Hayden's Ferry Review—"Psalm 137"
iO—"Beheaded Carcass of a Deer"
Iron Horse Literary Review—"Drawl"
Mead—"Killing a Rattler" (as "Grandpa Killing a Rattler")
Poet Lore—"Take, Eat" (as "Initiation")
Relief—"Pessimist's Guide to Miracles" and "Nicholas Copernicus"
Scythe—"Samson in Love" and "Deacons Meeting"
Southern Review—"Thanatophobia on Shinbone Valley Road"
Stirring—"Cozy Manor Personal Care Home, LaFayette, Georgia," and "Nicolas of Antioch, the Proselyte"
storySouth—"Persimmon"
Third Coast—"Isaiah"
Unsplendid—"Of Solomon" and "Orpheus in Huntsville, Alabama"

Heartfelt thanks to Eric Smith, Andrew Hudgins, and Chad Davidson, as well as Daniel Anderson, Henri Cole, Caitlin Doyle, Claudia Emerson, Alex Fabrizio, Kathy Fagan, Greg Fraser, Joshua Gottlieb-Miller, Mark Jarman, Thomas Lux, Emilia Phillips, Wyatt Prunty, Dave

Smith, Analicia Sotelo, Matt Sumpter, Sidney Wade, and G.C. Waldrep, without whose friendship, patience, generosity, and keen eyes and ears these poems would not have been possible.

Special thanks to Diane Goettel, Kit Frick, Angela Leroux-Lindsey, and the rest of the Black Lawrence Press team for their confidence in my work and for selecting this collection for the Black River Chapbook Competition.

I am grateful to the J. William Fulbright Program, the U.S. Department of State, the Bucknell Seminar for Younger Poets, the Sewanee Writers' Conference, the University of West Georgia, and The Ohio State University for the generous grants and fellowships that blessed me with the time and resources to bring these poems into being.

My undying love to my family.

Nick McRae is the author of *Mountain Redemption*, winner of the Fall 2011 Black River Chapbook Competition, as well the De Novo Prize-winning full-length *The Name Museum* (C&R Press, 2014). He is the editor of the anthology *Gathered: Contemporary Quaker Poets* (Sundress Publications, 2013). His poems, reviews, and translations appear in *Cincinnati Review, Hayden's Ferry Review, Linebreak, The Southern Review, Third Coast*, and elsewhere. He serves as associate editor for *32 Poems*, poetry coordinator for the annual *Best of the Net* anthology, and is a member of the Sewanee Writers' Conference staff. Born in Chattanooga, Tennessee, and raised in the Northwest Georgia foothills, Nick earned an M.F.A. in creative writing at The Ohio State University and is currently a Robert B. Toulouse Doctoral Fellow in English at the University of North Texas.